God Is

Salvation

For a Lost World

 THREE SKILLET

God Is

Salvation

For a Lost World

Volume 4

By
Farley Dunn

God Is Salvation for a Lost World /Farley Dunn – 1st ed.

Vol. 4

This is an original work created by
Farley Dunn for the website MyChurchNotes.net.

COPYRIGHT © 2015 BY FARLEY DUNN
www.mychurchnotes.net

All rights reserved.

ISBN: 978-1-943189-13-7

www.ThreeSkilletPublishing.com

Non-public domain scripture quotations are from The Holy Bible, English Standard Version® (ESV®), copyright © 2001 by Crossway, a publishing ministry of Good News Publishers. Used by permission. All rights reserved.

Dedication

To:

First Assembly of God
Azle, Texas

"I live by faith in the Son . . ."
Galatians 2:20

MyChurchNotes.net

Table of Contents

Almonds and Gold	19
Almost Saved	25
Becoming God's Thoroughbred	31
Caught in the Updraft	37
Death Walk	43
Drainpipe Effect	49
Empire State Christianity	55
Fanfare of God's Four Winds	61
Gifting Ourselves God	67
God's Family Ties	73
God's Seven Words	81
Good Cop, Bad Cop	87
I Am The Christ	93
No More Than a Flash of Light	99
Our Wake-up Call for Eternity	105
Soul Eater	111
Steel Spine Christianity	117
The Behold Factor	123
The Concrete Wall	129
The Knife Plunged Into Our Heart	135
The Story of Astonishing Wonders	141
Whiteboard of Truth	147
Coming to Christ in Three Easy Steps	153

Introduction

We live in a world that reaches out for God.

Sometimes the hurting people around us don't know why they are in pain, only that they are searching for something to fill the emptiness inside.

It is up to the Christian to reveal the truth of the cross in a manner that is appealing to those who see us walking at their side. If they are offended by our insensitivity, how will they find the cross of Jesus appealing?

This collection of 22 essays, each based on scripture from the Word of God, can provide that opening. Tell them of the truth in "Caught in the Updraft," or the depiction of the devil in "No More Than a Flash of Light," and you will get their attention. Mention "Soul Eater" or "The Story of Astonishing Wonders," and they will want to know more.

We don't have to beat the message of Christ into the unbeliever. We simply need to be interesting so that they will want to return for more. The more they find out about walking with Christ, the more they will desire him in their lives.

This book will provide you with scriptural truths to discuss with your neighbors and coworkers, and you will be able to offer them biblical nuggets of Christ's redeeming power presented in a new and fresh way.

Let's share God. When we are interesting, those around us will find God interesting.

Farley Dunn

Light Bulb Moment

All power comes from the Father, and Jesus is the conduit that channels it to us.

Almonds and Gold

Everyone can draw a flower. Put a circle in the middle, and attach five round petals.

There, we've drawn an almond flower.

Seen from the right angle, the petals of this beautiful bloom seem to form a cup. The bloom itself is white, fading to a deep pink in the center.

As beautiful as it is, there are more reasons why the almond tree is so significant in biblical lore. It is one of the first trees to bloom at the start of spring. In fact, the Hebrew word root for almond means to "watch" or "wake."

This is the tree that symbolizes an awakening, both from an earthly winter, and from our spiritual winter.

It is thought that both Aaron's rod and Jesus' cross may have been from almond wood. Numbers 17 tells the story of Aaron's rod budding, flowering, and producing almonds overnight. John J. Parsons relates the legend of the cross of Christ and how it budded after his death.

John D. Keyser believes Scripture substantiates the crucifixion taking place on a living tree. His reasoning? The Bible never mentions a cross, only the Messiah being hanged on a tree.

Could it have been an almond tree, the first tree in the land to bloom, indicating the end of winter and the arrival of spring?

After all, isn't that what Jesus did, came to bring new life to a world that was spiritually dead, just as the almond tree signifies new life to those suffering through a wintertime experience? Just as Aaron's rod signified the infusion of the power of the Almighty God?

In Jeremiah 1:11-12, Jeremiah's vision of the rod of an almond tree indicated God's promise to do all that he had promised the great prophet.

Let's put those three incidences together.

Almond Incident #1 – Aaron's Rod

> Aaron's rod budded, and the dissidents of the Korah rebellion were swallowed by the ground.

Almond Incident #2 – Jeremiah's Vision

Jeremiah viewed an almond rod, and God did all he said he would do. With haste, too.

Almond Incident #3 – The Messiah's Hanging Tree

Christ exploded upon the world, and men's lives were forever changed.

Is it any wonder the Menorah, the symbol of the "Tree of Life," is decorated with gold oil cups in the shape of almond blossoms? Exodus 25:31-40 tells of its construction. "You shall make a lampstand of pure gold . . . [with] cups made like almond blossoms . . ."

The almond tree represents life, in every way possible, from the innate and divine power of the Heavenly Father to the redemption brought down to earth by his son, Jesus.

John 1:14 tells us, "And the Word became flesh and dwelt among us, and we have seen his glory, glory as of the only Son from the Father, full of grace and truth."

Remember how easy it was to draw that almond flower? It is just as easy to come to Christ and accept him as Savior, Lord, and King.

All he wants us to do is ask and receive.

In summary, all power comes from the Father, and Jesus is the conduit that channels it to us.

Light Bulb Moment

Let's go for the sure thing. Let's invest in Jesus.

Almost Saved

We like to hedge our bets. The concept behind that is to get the best return for our money.

We've heard of mutual funds. We trust mutual funds to take risks on the stock market, but not so many that we might lose a substantial part of our investment.

We share that risk with thousands of others, spreading the potential losses.

A hedge fund is the same in one way: People share the risk. However, hedge funds take very, very big risks in hopes of very, very big rewards.

Or very big losses . . . which they hope to spread around across a wide segment of investors.

Hedging our bets: taking a risk in hopes it will pay off with a sweet paycheck in the end.

Do we hedge our bets as Christians? Do we take risks,

hoping we make heaven our eternal home, but we're not quite willing to make a full commitment?

Matthew 5:27-28 tells us, "You have heard that it was said, 'You shall not commit adultery.' But I say to you that everyone who looks at a woman with lustful intent has already committed adultery with her in his heart."

Hedging our bets . . . hoping our look won't skewer our salvation.

Matthew 6:24 explains that "No one can serve two masters, for either he will hate the one and love the other, or he will be devoted to the one and despise the other. You cannot serve God and money."

Hedging our bets . . . hoping our money won't become our master.

Matthew 5:46-47 cautions us, "For if you love those who love you, what reward do you have? Do not even the tax collectors do the same? And if you greet only your brothers, what more are you doing than others? Do not even the Gentiles do the same?"

Hedging our bets . . . hoping our displays of affection won't become our decimation of affliction.

Matthew 7:3 says, "Why do you see the speck that is in your brother's eye, but do not notice the log that is in your own eye?"

Hedging our bets . . . hoping our self-centered uprightness won't become our spiritual undoing.

Is it worth the risk? Really?

Hedge fund investors are a heady lot, with audacious nerve and veins of steel. They want that adrenalin rush of success, and they are willing to risk total failure along the way.

We don't want to walk up to the pearly gates, only to have God say to us, "Oh, I'm sorry. You're almost saved, but those were some really risky behaviors you took."

We can't hedge our bets and still make it into heaven.

In summary, let's go for the sure thing. Let's invest in Jesus.

Light Bulb Moment

When we give control to God, he trains us to run as a thoroughbred for him.

Becoming God's Thoroughbred

Horses are among the most beautiful of God's creatures. We envision them standing in the wind, mane and tail blowing free; or running on the beach, with water splashing at each footstep. Who would not love horses, for they embody elegance and power.

Yet, and there is always a yet, as beautiful as a horse is, it only becomes useful when it is willing to accept a bridle, showing it submits to our authority. The thoroughbred racer? It will amount to nothing if left to run free in the field. A child's pony? It will buck wildly if not trained to accept a rider. A cutting horse? No one wins a competition on an untrained beast.

James 3:2 tells us:

> "For we all stumble in many ways. And if anyone does not stumble in what he says, he is a perfect man, able also to bridle his whole body."

The bridle is the Lord's, and when we submit to him, we will walk with a sure step, a thoroughbred in him.

Why is accepting the bridle of the Lord so vital to Christian living? Look at these examples:

Proverbs 25:23 gives us cause to think:

> "The north wind brings forth rain, and a backbiting tongue, angry looks."

Leviticus 19:16 warns us against the path of the unbridled person:

> "You shall not go around as a slanderer among your people, and you shall not stand up against the life of your neighbor: I am the Lord."

Revelation 21:8 opens the book to our fate if we refuse the bridle of the Lord:

> "But as for the cowardly, the faithless, the detestable, as for murderers, the sexually immoral, sorcerers, idolaters, and all liars, their portion will be in the lake that burns with fire and sulfur, which is the second death."

If we return to the first chapter of James, in Verse 19, we are given the first gentle nudge that helps us to accept our bridle:

> "Know this, my beloved brothers: let every per-

son be quick to hear, slow to speak, slow to anger . . ."

As humans, we love standing in the wind, and to run the beach with water underneath our feet, who would not enjoy that? Yet, we can become God's thoroughbred only when we accept his constraints. We will provide help to the weak only when we give up our freedoms to him. We will divide the Word of Truth only when we allow Christ to train us with his skillful hand.

In summary, when we give control to God, he trains us to run as a thoroughbred for him.

Light Bulb Moment

Jesus lifts us up, and we cannot fall as long as we trust in him.

Caught in the Updraft

Alpine swifts are birds that can do something few other birds can: remain in flight for up to six months at a time.

Truly, they never land. They eat on wing, drink on wing, and for their first two or three years of life, don't nest.

They remain caught in the updraft, even sleeping on wing. If they lose the wind under their wings, they will tumble to the ground and risk impending death.

How as Christians can we remain caught in the updraft?

John 3:16, that oh-so-familiar verse, tells us:

> "For God so loved the world, that he gave his only Son, that whoever believes in him should not perish but have eternal life."

This is the source of our updraft. God's love lifts us

above the turmoil of everyday living, and he keeps us in daily flight. As long as we trust in him, we will never fall from the sky.

John 10:30 tells us:

"I and the Father are one."

If we can find our faith in Jesus, we can have faith in God, for there is no difference. When we accept Jesus as our savior, we have invited God to be our continual gust of spiritual upwelling, and we need never touch land again.

John 1:18 tells us:

"No one has ever seen God; the only God, who is at the Father's side, he has made him known."

Naysayers will tell us we cannot soar on wing, because there is nothing to hold us up. Yet, we cannot see the air beneath the Alpine swift's wing, only the effects of what it does. God is the same. We cannot see him, only the effects of what he does, and what he does is keep us aloft, always and ever closer to him.

John 1:14 tells us:

"And the Word became flesh and dwelt among us, and we have seen his glory, glory as of the only Son from the Father, full of grace and truth."

God understands us more than we think. He and Jesus are one, and Jesus came to earth to live as flesh that he might know us as we are. Jesus also had to remain caught in the updrafts of his Father's love, just as we do, so that he could bring us redemption for our souls. He did this against the taunts of his own people turned against him, the temptations of the devil at his lowest points, and a horrifying death many of us cannot even imagine.

How does the Alpine swift manage its amazing feat? It just leaps. It doesn't look at the rocks far below and consider whether it should. It just does it.

Let's leap toward God, and when we trust in him, we will become caught in the updraft of his love.

In summary, Jesus lifts us up, and we cannot fall as long as we trust in him.

Light Bulb Moment

Our body might die, but our soul will live forever. Let's make sure we pay attention to where we will spend eternity.

Death Walk

Let's ask the question: How can a living, breathing person also be dead?

We're not talking about zombies, either. So, let's ask the question again. How can a living, breathing human also be dead? Especially, and this is important, if he or she is walking around as a normal person would.

Those alive in the middle of the 20th century will remember the Bataan Death March. In 1942 the Japanese force-marched tens of thousands of American and Filipino POWs upwards of 80 miles through tropical heat. They were given no food or water, and those who fell were bayonetted or beheaded.

The moment they started out, these men considered themselves on a death walk. The chances of survival in those conditions were slim to none.

Those who made it to their destination fared little better. They were not given food for three days after their arrival, and they continued to die at the rate of 50 per day.

That's old news, some might say. It was war time, and that could never happen again.

Yet, it is happening even as we read this. People are on a death walk right now, and they are people we know, people we work with, perhaps even people we are married to.

Ephesians 2:1-2 tells us we "were dead in the trespasses and sins in which [we] once walked, following the course of this world, following the prince of the power of the air, the spirit that is now at work in the sons of disobedience."

We were alive and dead at the same time. Oh, our physical bodies breathed in air and moved when our brains told our muscles to carry us hither and yon. However, our spirits were already dead, for there was no hope for our redemption.

Then the Father of all creation intervened. Genesis 1:1 tells us: "In the beginning, God created the heavens and the earth." He gave life to all creation. Then, when his creation was on a death walk to hell, our Father gave us life again.

He gave us Jesus.

As John 10:28 relates in Jesus' own words: "And I give unto them eternal life; and they shall never perish, neither shall any man pluck them out of my hand."

We are on a death walk when we walk in the world. We walk in life when we walk with Jesus. Which is better? Read the tales of the survivors of the Bataan Death March.

The devil makes the world seem attractive, but the end result is the same. Let's be smart. Let's choose life. Let's choose Jesus.

In summary, our body might die, but our soul will live forever. Let's make sure we pay attention to where we will spend eternity.

Light Bulb Moment

We must fall into Jesus, for he will guide us where we need to go.

Drainpipe Effect

Visit Los Angeles, a place for sun and fun. Yet, the inhabitants of that city need rain just as much as those in any other city in the United States. In fact, without it, they cannot survive. Los Angeles is a desert city, and without rain, the people will suffer and die.

Yet, too much rain too quickly is equally deadly. The answer is to build drainpipes. Even the Los Angeles River has been subjugated to drainpipe status.

What do drainpipes do for us? They control the influx of water, sending the flood just the direction we want it to go.

We can call it the Drainpipe Effect.

The Drainpipe Effect is fully functional in Christianity, also. Check out these proofs from the Word of God:

Matthew 7:13-14 tells us:

> "Enter by the narrow gate. For the gate is wide and

the way is easy that leads to destruction, and those who enter by it are many. For the gate is narrow and the way is hard that leads to life, and those who find it are few."

Those who miss the Drainpipe are the destructive flood that covers the land, washing away morals and right living, and leaving desolation in their wake. We must channel ourselves in Jesus to reach our heavenly home.

Matthew 6:33 is our signpost:

"But seek first the kingdom of God and his righteousness, and all these things will be added to you."

The Drainpipe is there for all to see. Even so, we must look for it if we want the Father to guide and direct us on the course to him.

John 8:24 cautions us:

"I told you that you would die in your sins, for unless you believe that I am he you will die in your sins."

If we try any other way except Jesus, we will miss the Drainpipe altogether, and we will wither in the deserts of this world.

We live in a world full of people who are headed

somewhere. They are as a drenching rain covering the surface of the earth, falling to the ground and cascading where they will throughout the days of their lives. Only those who fall into the Jesus Drainpipe will eventually find their desired goal: safety in the arms of the Christ.

That's the Drainpipe Effect in a nutshell. It's falling into Jesus, heart and soul, and letting ourselves be swept away by him, with no regard for the cares of this world.

In summary, we must fall into Jesus, for he will guide us where we need to go.

Light Bulb Moment

When we build for Jesus, we build for the long term. Let's build well.

Empire State Christianity

The Empire State Building in New York City was built at one of the lowest times in America's history.

The final stages of planning came together in 1929, one of the most prosperous times in America's history. The Stock Market was running at an all-time high, and money was pouring in hand over fist. All someone had to do was walk down Wall Street to become rich, some quipped at the time.

By the start of excavation in January 1930, America was in a downward economic spiral. Even so, construction went ahead full steam. The building was finished months ahead of schedule, to a celebratory opening in May 1931. Due to its lack of tenants, it was sometimes called the "Empty State Building."

The Empire State Building did not become profitable until 1950. Today it is one of the most iconic structures in the world, and in 2011, after a major renovation, it received a gold Leadership in Energy and

Environmental Design rating, the tallest building in the United States to earn this prestigious award.

All this from a building that many considered a failure at the onset of construction.

What obstacles do we face in the construction of our Christian lives? Are we poor? Divorced? Molested as children? Or do we come from a background where money is considered more important than God? What keeps our Christian edifice from rising high above the people around us, and becoming a beacon of inspiration to the entire world?

Romans 12:1 gives us our construction plans:

> "I appeal to you therefore, brothers, by the mercies of God, to present your bodies as a living sacrifice, holy and acceptable to God, which is your spiritual worship."

2 Peter 1:1 reminds us of our foundations:

> "Simeon Peter, a servant and apostle of Jesus Christ, To those who have obtained a faith of equal standing with ours by the righteousness of our God and Savior Jesus Christ:"

Romans 12:2 assures us the world's downturns don't dictate our building schedule:

> "Do not be conformed to this world, but be transformed by the renewal of your mind, that by testing you may discern what is the will of God, what is good and acceptable and perfect."

Mark 13:1-5 warns us that only our spiritual edifices will endure:

> "And as he came out of the temple, one of his disciples said to him, 'Look, Teacher, what wonderful stones and what wonderful buildings!' And Jesus said to him, 'Do you see these great buildings? There will not be left here one stone upon another that will not be thrown down.' And as he sat on the Mount of Olives opposite the temple, Peter and James and John and Andrew asked him privately, 'Tell us, when will these things be, and what will be the sign when all these things are about to be accomplished?' And Jesus began to say to them, 'See that no one leads you astray.' "

When we begin on our Christian walk, others may look at us and see only the failures we have made. When we toss off the world's encumbrances to make room for Christ as our foundation stone, they may see only an empty hole. However, even if it takes twenty years for Christ to turn us around into the Christian he wishes us to be, there is one thing we must always keep in mind.

People loved the Empire State Building even when it was an empty shell, tenantless and unprofitable. The proof? In the first year it brought in more money from the observation deck than from rent.

When we build our Empire State Building, we have to discount the naysayers, look to the future, and continually strive to be the best we can be. Then we will become an iconic standard for Jesus, and he will make his mark on the world through us.

In summary, when we build for Jesus, we build for the long term. Let's build well.

Light Bulb Moment

When Jesus blows his trumpet, all creation will come running.

Fanfare of God's Four Winds

A diaspora is a scattering of many parts. Think of the dandelion. It grows a puffball or "blowball" of seeds specially designed to break up in the slightest breeze and be carried aloft by the wind. Once it's gone, it's gone. Who could ever bring a dandelion blowball back together again?

God's Chosen are that dandelion. They matured into a great nation from a single seed, the great patriarch Abraham. Then, a worldly puff of air pressed against the beautiful thing God had created, and in a moment of time, his People were scattered as far as the east is from the west.

The modern Christian church is the same. We sprang from the one seed of Jesus, and under the auspices of God's watchful eye, we blossomed into something wonderful. God needed more, though, and with the breath of his lungs, he scattered his faithful throughout the earth to bear his seed unto all nations.

He is ready to call us home.

Isaiah 11:12 tells us of the gathering in of his Chosen:

> "He will raise a signal for the nations and will assemble the banished of Israel, and gather the dispersed of Judah from the four corners of the earth."

Many modern scholars believe this happened in 1948 with the creation of the Jewish state in Israel. God's People flocked to their Promised Land from places as varied as New Jersey, Argentina, and Canada.

Jesus made a call long before that, though, one that was a spiritual plea to the Jews. We read his words in John 14:6, where Jesus speaks to Thomas:

> "Jesus said to him, 'I am the way, and the truth, and the life. No one comes to the Father except through me.'"

Jesus hoped to gather his banished Children from the four corners of the earth, and draw them back unto God. When they rejected him, his gentile blowball of seeds (his disciples) exploded beneath the winds of the Roman overlords, carrying his message of hope and redemption to all the world.

Soon his trumpet will sound, and we will be called home. 1 Thessalonians 4:16 describes the upcoming

Fanfare of God's Four Winds that will be our signal that the time is come:

> "For the Lord himself will descend from heaven with a cry of command, with the voice of an archangel, and with the sound of the trumpet of God."

This passage continues to tell us the dead in Christ will be caught up first, then those who are still alive will gather with him, also. What a glorious day that will be!

God can indeed draw the dandelion back together once again, for all power in heaven and on earth is his. Our job is to continue to be an example in all we do in order to draw others unto him in preparation for that day.

In summary, when Jesus blows his trumpet, all creation will come running!

Light Bulb Moment

When we want to give ourselves a really good gift, let's open up the Jesus package. It's the best one out there.

Gifting Ourselves God

It's Christmas morning, and as we open our eyes from sleep, we groan at the thought.

Not quite the expected beginning, is it?

Still, back to the story. The lights of the tree twinkle through the open doorway, reflected in the family portraits hung in the hallway. We can hear excited voices in a distant room, exclaiming over what each person has received.

What's in it for us? We were up at two assembling Bobby's bike, and to wrap Mary's electric piano? Who could have predicted the nightmare there?

What's under the tree for us, we wonder. Aunt Shirley's fruitcake and a tie from Uncle Ralph? Is there anything exciting in there at all, for us, we mean, a gift we actually want to open?

That question shifts our story a little bit, because what gift do we actually want?

A man once quipped, "If it's something I really want, you can't afford it, anyway. So, don't bother. I'll just get it myself."

For many of us, there's a core of truth in that statement.

So, we're back to our question. What do we really want? What's the gift that's so big it overshadows all other gifts, one that is so valuable that no one gathered around the tree in the other room has the funds to buy it, and we can only hope beyond hope that it will someday be ours?

After the two-word verse that tells of Jesus' sorrow, John 3:16 is the most recognized set of words in the Bible.

> "For God so loved the world, that he gave his only Son, that whoever believes in him should not perish but have eternal life."

Now about that gift . . . no one in the other room may have the financial acumen to gift us the best gift in the world, but someone does.

Hebrews 9:27 gives us a frightful assessment of our future:

> "And just as it is appointed for man to die once, and after that comes judgment."

Well, it would be frightful if not for the following assurance:

> "For God so loved the world, that he gave his only Son, that whoever believes in him should not perish but have eternal life."

Is this hitting home, yet? If we want the best gift around, God has already bought and paid for it. It's already under the tree. When we open that package, it will be filled with salvation, freedom from the sin that keeps us bound, and eternal life through Christ Jesus, our Risen Lord.

So, throw those sheets back and leap from that bed. Don't even bother getting dressed. Run to the tree in those pajamas and search for the gift we want to give ourselves.

Let's run to Jesus.

In summary, when we want to give ourselves a really good gift, let's open up the Jesus package. It's the best one out there.

Light Bulb Moment

Becoming part of Jesus' family gives us power and authority that surpasses that of the world.

God's Family Ties

The phrase "Blood is thicker than water" is indelibly etched into modern culture.

What it says is that those who are related to us are more important than those who are not. Essentially, if two people ask us for money, and one is related, and the other is not, we will give the money to the one with blood ties.

This is not always a good thing. Take the gangsters of the Roaring Twenties. They called up favors by the means of family relationships. There may have been five major "families" in New York's Italian Mafia, but in Chicago alone, by the mid-1920s, there were an estimated 1,300 gangs spread throughout the city. Many of these were made up of brothers, fathers, and others who carried blood ties.

Outside of Chicago, we recognize these names: Bonnie and Clyde, killed in May 1934 in Texas; and "Doc" and "Ma" Barker and her son Fred, killed in Florida in

January 1935.

In Columbia, Juan Pablo Escobar and "Uncle" Joe Ochoa ran Medellin's criminal side with an iron fist. The Kray brothers of London mixed with Judy Garland, Frank Sinatra, and Diana Dors. They also spread intimidation, leading their gang in armed robberies, arson, protection rackets, and decidedly vicious murders.

Let's look at two groups to see how family ties brought about some of these similar results in the Bible.

Acts 4:6 lists the members of a highly placed Family.

> "With Annas the high priest and Caiaphas and John and Alexander, and all who were of the high-priestly family."

Family. Blood. John 18:13 reveals that Annas was the father-in-law of Caiaphas, who was high priest that year. These are the ties that bind a group together and cause them to make decisions that they might not otherwise make. At this point in history, those ties were about to initiate intimidation and a robbery.

The Family causes intimidation:

Matthew 26:47 is set in the garden of Gethsemane.

> "While he was still speaking, Judas came, one of

the twelve, and with him a great crowd with swords and clubs, from the chief priests and the elders of the people."

The chief priests and elders sent this mob, consisting of men carrying swords and clubs, to strike fear into the disciples' hearts. If they had wanted Jesus, they could have taken him at any time. Instead, they wanted their fist to be felt among those who knew Jesus best. Then, his followers would crumble when Jesus was crushed.

The Family sparks robbery:

Matthew 27:3-5 reveals the story of a life stolen for mere greed.

> "Then when Judas, his betrayer, saw that Jesus was condemned, he changed his mind and brought back the thirty pieces of silver to the chief priests and the elders, saying, 'I have sinned by betraying innocent blood.' They said, 'What is that to us? See to it yourself.' And throwing down the pieces of silver into the temple, he departed, and he went and hanged himself."

Whatever we may think of Judas, he was distraught at the outcome of his actions. The Family didn't care. Their concern was for their ultimate goal, which was control over their perceived domain. By their callus response, they robbed Judas of a life that could have been made new by the forgiving hand of the Almighty God.

Yet there was another Family who had power, and they were banded together to protect their own. Let's see how their tight-knit hold on power brought about a protection racket and a decidedly vicious murder.

The Family sells protection:

John 18:31 is the Jews' safety net.

> "Pilate said to them, 'Take him yourselves and judge him by your own law.' The Jews said to him, 'It is not lawful for us to put anyone to death.' "

The Family placed the blame for Jesus' crucifixion on the Romans' shoulders, rather than accept it on their own. They thought they were providing spiritual protection for the entire Jewish race. In spite of their undercover machinations, in John 19:11, Jesus places the blame squarely where it belongs, telling Pilate that the Jews shoulder the entire blame, no matter who orders his death.

The Family promotes murder:

> Mark 15:25 tells us about the day that brought eternal infamy upon the Jews.

"And it was the third hour when they crucified him."

Jesus could have been set free. We know from the written Word that this was not the plan of God, but the Family had it in their power. Instead, they chose to take out their opposition, insisting that he be plastered to a cross and left to die underneath a cruel sky. It was vicious murder at the very worst level.

Blood is thicker than water. It is the tie that binds. That is exactly why Jesus had to die on that long-ago cross. His shed blood makes us one with him, and in his death and resurrection, we are now part of his family. What he asks of us, we readily give. When he needs us to go, we do not question. We trust him in all things, and nothing else takes precedence over our relationship with him.

In summary, becoming part of Jesus' family gives us power and authority that surpasses that of the world.

Light Bulb Moment

God loves us, and he will continue to encourage us to come to him until we take the time to stop and listen.

God's Seven Words

In teaching a child, educators are told to rephrase, rephrase, and rephrase. If a child doesn't get it the first time we say it, find a different way to get the message across.

Repeating the same message the child didn't get the first time doesn't help the struggling learner absorb it the next six times.

We are the children God wants to teach. He wants us to learn his lessons so much that he takes the time to tell us over and over what he wants us to know.

Here are seven words from the mouth of God:

Romans 5:8 tells us:

> "But God shows his love for us in that while we were still sinners, Christ died for us."

In yet different words, we read in John 3:16:

> "For God so loved the world, that he gave his only

Son, that whoever believes in him should not perish but have eternal life."

Revelation 21:4 shares the same riveting message:

> "He will wipe away every tear from their eyes, and death shall be no more, neither shall there be mourning, nor crying, nor pain anymore, for the former things have passed away."

1 John 4:8 restates God's position:

> "Anyone who does not love does not know God, because God is love."

Titus 1:2 hopes we finally understand:

> "In hope of eternal life, which God, who never lies, promised before the ages began . . ."

1 Corinthians 6:9 is yet another way God makes his point:

> "Or do you not know that the unrighteous will not inherit the kingdom of God? Do not be deceived: neither the sexually immoral, nor idolaters, nor adulterers . . ."

Romans 3:23 nudges us one more time to the truth:

> "For all have sinned and fall short of the glory of God . . ."

All of these tell us the same thing in seven different ways. God loves us; he sent his Son to die for us; and he wants us to live a blameless life for him. All he needs us to do is listen and follow his plan. He's written it down. We call it the Word of God.

In summary, God loves us, and he will continue to encourage us to come to him until we take the time to stop and listen.

Light Bulb Moment

When we choose Jesus, we've made the good choice.

Good Cop, Bad Cop

Hold up one hand. Look at both sides. It has a front, and it has a back. Yet, both are on the same hand. We can't look at one side and say, "You are good. I will keep you," and turn our hand, only to say, "You are bad. I do not want you."

It's like a criminal interrogation. Two cops are in the interview room. One plays the authoritarian, no-nonsense stickler, and the other offers to bring the interviewee a cup of coffee. A strategy is in place, Good Cop, Bad Cop, in order to effectively win the trust of the suspect.

The guy in the chair can't look at one cop and say, "You are good. I'll keep you," and turn to the other cop and say, "You are bad. I don't want you." The two are a team. When we have one, we have the other. They are a pair. We can only choose which one we will align with.

Good and bad in this world are the same. We will

have good, and we will have bad. We cannot say, "I will keep only good things around me, and I want the bad things to go away." The world doesn't respond to our desires that way. We can only choose which we will align with.

Ezekiel 18:20 gives us a clear example of this principle:

> "The soul who sins shall die. The son shall not suffer for the iniquity of the father, nor the father suffer for the iniquity of the son. The righteousness of the righteous shall be upon himself, and the wickedness of the wicked shall be upon himself."

> We have a choice. Good. Bad. Both are there; both will continue to be there. We have to decide where our affinity lies, and we will receive consequences—good or bad—in line with our deeds.

1 Timothy 1:8-10 encourages us not to discount the advice of our forebears:

> "Now we know that the law is good, if one uses it lawfully, understanding this, that the law is not laid down for the just but for the lawless and disobedient, for the ungodly and sinners, for the unholy and profane, for those who strike their fathers and mothers, for murderers, the sexually immoral, men who practice homosexuality, enslav-

ers, liars, perjurers, and whatever else is contrary to sound doctrine."

We can find wisdom in the advice of those who have gone before us. Our duty is to use it wisely, determining what is of good quality, and what is not. The laws we have on the books are to encourage those without direction to walk after the Lord.

Matthew 7:1-2 advises us to be careful in our view of others.

"Judge not, that you be not judged. For with the judgment you pronounce you will be judged, and with the measure you use it will be measured to you."

When we choose what's good, and others are still struggling with Good Cop, Bad Cop, we must be patient with them. Just as Christ called us gently until we were ready to make a decision for him, so must we be patient with those who still feel his call, even if their readiness to move after him is unclear to us.

1 Thessalonians 4:16-18 is the voice of our Victory Cry!

"For the Lord himself will descend from heaven with a cry of command, with the voice of an archangel, and with the sound of the trumpet of God. And the dead in Christ will rise first. Then we who are alive, who are left, will be caught up together with them in the clouds to meet the Lord in the air, and so we will always be with the Lord. Therefore encourage one another with these words."

Good will win out over bad. God will win over the devil. Christ will triumph over sinful man.

In this life, we will face the challenges of good and evil, for we will always have both with us. That we cannot change. Our responsibility is to look at both and say, "I choose you," and to make sure our finger is pointed at the good cop. After all, the good cop is Jesus, and he's the one who'll bring us that steaming cup of coffee—which is our salvation at the cross, by the way!

In summary, when we choose Jesus, we've made the good choice.

Light Bulb Moment

When we want to be sure, we want Jesus. When he says he is the Christ, all creation backs him up.

I Am The Christ

Pull out a credit card. Yes, a credit card. Look in the bottom corner, and we'll see our name boldly embossed in the plastic. When we're using our plastic, we want people to know who we are. We can even get custom cards with our alma mater or our grandchildren pasted right on the front.

Look at me, it screams, making sure we're us; and we willingly pull out our ID cards to show we are who we say we are. We have the right to use our card.

It's all about proving our identity. If someone else uses our card, we want someone to notice. They've stolen our identity, and we want them held accountable. If they charge up bills in our name, we cry, "I am the real me! They are a fake! Can't you tell?"

Matthew 7:15 starts off with:

> "Beware of false prophets, who come to you in sheep's clothing but inwardly are ravenous wolves..."

The false prophets claim to have their names on the resurrection of the King, but we know better. Only Jesus can make that boast.

2 Peter 2:15 tells us:

> "Forsaking the right way, they have gone astray. They have followed the way of Balaam . . ."

> Balaam didn't give his life on the cross. Only Jesus can brag, "I am the Christ, and all men must come through me!"

Revelation 21:8 makes man's claims to truth transparent:

> "But as for the cowardly, the faithless, the detestable, as for murderers, the sexually immoral, sorcerers, idolaters, and all liars, their portion will be in the lake that burns with fire and sulfur, which is the second death."

> God will hold those accountable who use his name for their own purposes.

Identity thieves in this world often live well for a time. Bernie Madoff, Charles Ponzi, and even Sarah Howe in 1880, who offered an investment opportunity strictly for women, only to disappear into obscurity with the funds. Yet, they weren't the savvy investors they claimed. They offered something false, and their investors lost everything.

Jesus is our ultimate investment. When he says, "I am the Christ," we can take it to the bank, confident our souls are secure.

The Word breathes truth we can depend on in Acts 4:12:

> "And there is salvation in no one else, for there is no other name under heaven given among men by which we must be saved."

In summary, when we want to be sure, we want Jesus. When he says he is the Christ, all creation backs him up.

Light Bulb Moment

When we continually watch Jesus, we won't notice the devil as he flashes out of our presence, farther away than the most distant heavenly bodies.

No More Than a Flash of Light

A beam of light travels at 186,000 miles per second. Not per hour, but per second. That's 3,600 times faster than 186,000 miles per hour.

Light is here, and it's gone.

So, when we say something is gone in a flash, it's 186,000 miles away in one second. It's here, and then it's gone, and it's so far away it cannot affect us anymore, at all, ever again. We are free of it.

What do we need to be free of? Whatever it is, when we give it to God, it becomes no more than a flash of light, and it is immediately cast from us as far as the ends of the earth are from each other.

Farther, in fact. The earth is only 8,000 miles through the center and 24,000 miles around the equator. When we give something to God, it's not even on this earth to come back and haunt us.

2 Corinthians 11:14 tells us that:

> ". . . Satan disguises himself as an angel of light."

That statement has two meanings. The first is that at first appearance, Satan is beautiful. The second is that just like a beam of light, if we ignore him, he flashes on by at a breakneck speed, and he is gone from us, no more than a flash of brilliance to be forgotten, because at that speed, in one second he is no longer on the face of the earth. He is out of our sight, kaput, sayonara, and the least of our worries.

Rather, let's focus on God.

1 John 2:2 gives us our first bit of good news:

> "He is the propitiation for our sins, and not for ours only but also for the sins of the whole world."

> This is exactly what the devil tries to distract us from. He doesn't want us to see the true Christ.

2 Peter 3:9 is our assurance that we will find Jesus when we reach out to him:

> "The Lord is not slow to fulfill his promise as some count slowness, but is patient toward you, not wishing that any should perish, but that all should reach repentance."

When we remove the sunglasses of sin, we will see the shining light of the Father above.

Ephesians 2:8-9 tells us how easy it is to come to him:

> "For by grace you have been saved through faith. And this is not your own doing; it is the gift of God, not a result of works, so that no one may boast."

> It's like flipping the switch on a flashlight. The light is just there.

Hebrews 6:1 lines out how we can be assured we will never again be distracted by Satan:

> "Therefore let us leave the elementary doctrine of Christ and go on to maturity, not laying again a foundation of repentance from dead works and of faith toward God."

> He is our power source, and by trusting in him, his Holy Light shining through us will never be dimmed.

The devil is a flash of brilliance that fades as soon as he distracts us from the Holy Presence of God Almighty. However, Jesus is the switch that turns up the power, and against the awe-inspiring brilliance of God, we cannot see Satan's wimpy light anywhere around us. It comes, and it's gone, no more than a flash of light that has nothing to do with us.

In summary, when we continually watch Jesus, we won't notice the devil as he flashes out of our presence, farther away than the most distant heavenly bodies.

Light Bulb Moment

If we sleep through the rising of the sun, we will miss the breaking of God's new dawn.

Our Wake-up Call for Eternity

All good hotels do it. Some phone companies provide this service. We can even subscribe to plans that will notify us of impending events, down to the time we need to wake each morning.

We have a wakeup call about to ring forth across the whole earth. God has provided the contract, the pending schedule, and the method of delivery.

Genesis 11:6-9 changed man's plans:

> "And the Lord said, 'Behold . . . nothing that they propose to do will now be impossible for them. . . . And from there the Lord dispersed them over the face of all the earth."

Joshua 1:1-2 revealed a new direction for God's people:

> "After the death of Moses the servant of the Lord,

the Lord said to Joshua the son of Nun, Moses' assistant, 'Moses my servant is dead. Now therefore arise, go over this Jordan, you and all this people, into the land that I am giving to them...'"

Luke 18:8 tells us to think differently:

"I tell you, he will give justice to them speedily. Nevertheless, when the Son of Man comes, will he find faith on earth?"

Psalm 19:4-6 reveals all that we are:

"Their voice goes out through all the earth, and their words to the end of the world. . . . There is nothing hidden from [him]."

1 Thessalonians 4:16 is the End of Days:

"For the Lord himself will descend from heaven with a cry of command, with the voice of an archangel, and with the sound of the trumpet of God. And the dead in Christ will rise first."

What wakeup call have we subscribed to? Or have we decided to sleep in, risking the chance that we will miss God's trumpet call?

We can read in Isaiah 13:13 of the one that brings us his eternal majesty in the day of our final awakening:

"Therefore I will make the heavens tremble, and the earth will be shaken out of its place, at the wrath of the Lord of hosts in the day of his fierce anger."

In summary, if we sleep through the rising of the sun, we will miss the breaking of God's new dawn.

Light Bulb Moment

God gives us life. Let's not offer it freely to the devil.

Soul Eater

For things to live, they must consume food.

To a tree, that means drawing water and nutrients from the soil so that sunlight can convert them into food in the leaves. Remove the water and nutrients, and the tree dies.

Some living creatures draw their nourishment directly from other living things in their ecosphere. We call them parasites. Separate them, and the parasite dies.

Humans and other mammals, as well as birds and other creatures . . . what about them? Where do they get their food in order to live?

The local Piggly Wiggly is certainly a valid choice, but at a more primal level, it comes from the plants and animals all around us. Remove those from our reach, and we will eventually die.

If we eat the wrong foods, we will achieve the same

result. We will eventually die, becoming no more than a food source for yet other creatures, including the bacteria that turns our bodies back into the dust of the earth.

We have to make good choices. Yet, what about feeding our spiritual man? How does all that work?

Let's look at three steps in the process, all of which lead to an inescapable fact: If we don't watch out, we will become a food source for yet another hungry creature.

Step 1: God makes us.

> Genesis 2:7 is the beginning of Man's story. This is where life sprang into being; where we made the transition from inanimate matter into living flesh; where the "magic" happened.
>
> "Then the Lord God formed the man of dust from the ground and breathed into his nostrils the breath of life, and the man became a living creature."
>
> From Genesis 2:7 on, Man walks and talks.

Step 2: Man makes a choice.

> 1 John 1:9 tells us the core process of our decision to live or die in the spiritual realm. This is where life springs into being; where we make the transi-

tion from death to life; where the spiritual man begins to walk with God.

"If we confess our sins, he is faithful and just to forgive us our sins and to cleanse us from all unrighteousness."

While the Word tells us all manner of ways we can tweak our Christian walk to improve our relationship with him, from this point, we are alive in Jesus.

Step 3: The devil makes a meal of us.

Ezekiel 18:4, 20 and Romans 6:23 show how making the incorrect choice feeds the Soul Eater. After all, a parasite has to have a food source, also. It cannot make its own food. The only way it can live is to draw its nourishment directly from others in its environment.

If we choose to inhabit the devil's environment, he will use us for a food source.

"The soul who sins shall die . . . and the wickedness of the wicked shall be upon himself."

"Behold, all souls are mine; . . . the soul who sins shall die."

"For the wages of sin is death . . ."

We have a solution. We don't have to be a food source for the devil. We don't have to feed him our souls.

Matthew 10:28 tells us we should ". . . fear him who can destroy both soul and body in hell," not chum up with him on Saturday night. The devil shouldn't be our friend.

Rather, we should do as Colossians 3:5 and Galatians 5:16 tell us. If we want to live, it is imperative to "put to death therefore what is earthly in you . . ." and ". . . walk by the Spirit . . ." so that we might not become part of the devil's daily smorgasbord.

In summary, God gives us life. Let's not offer it freely to the devil.

Light Bulb Moment

Jesus is ahead; let's not look any other direction.

Steel Spine Christianity

Have you ever seen someone who's had a broken back, and they've had to have multiple vertebrae fused? Maybe they've got a steel rod down their spine, and they can no longer twist and turn to look to the side or behind them.

We wouldn't wish that on anyone in the flesh. But in the spirit, that's exactly what God wants to do for us. He wants to open us up, implant a steel rod in our lives, and give us the backbone to always face forward, without looking to the side or behind us. He wants to fuse our vertebrae forever facing him so that there is no thought of turning away from his mercy and grace.

Let's see what God's Word says about walking in his Steel Spine Christianity:

Acts 2:38 is our surgical operation:

> "And Peter said to them, 'Repent and be baptized every one of you in the name of Jesus Christ for

the forgiveness of your sins, and you will receive the gift of the Holy Spirit.' "

Revelation 12:11 is the surgeon's guarantee of success:

"And they have conquered him by the blood of the Lamb and by the word of their testimony, for they loved not their lives even unto death."

James 1:5 tells us God is on call if we stumble:

"If any of you lacks wisdom, let him ask God, who gives generously to all without reproach, and it will be given him."

Titus 2:4 says the plan is for everyone:

"And so train the young women to love their husbands and children."

2 Timothy 3:16-17 is our billboard ad that invites others to God's surgery:

"All Scripture is breathed out by God and profitable for teaching, for reproof, for correction, and for training in righteousness, that the man of God may be competent, equipped for every good work."

Sure, our steel spine and our fused vertebrae limit our motion. We can't turn aside to see every distraction of the devil, and that's a good thing. We also can't look back at the life we left behind. We must face forward, and that's well and good, because that's where Jesus will be found.

In summary, Jesus is ahead; let's not look any other direction.

Light Bulb Moment

When our words come from Jesus, they carry power we could never speak on our own.

The Behold Factor

Blending into the background isn't possible for some of us. We're going to shine with flash and bling no matter how hard we try otherwise.

We walk through the door, and the spotlights turn our direction; the band strikes up the music, and our very presence shouts, "Behold! Look who's walked into the room!"

Anyone who's spent time with a "behold" person knows the feeling. They exude a presence that's bigger than they are. They seem to take over, even when they don't mean to. It's natural and uncontrollable.

It's part of who they are, their Behold Factor, so to speak. It just comes out, and they don't even have to say anything for us to feel it.

That's how God is. He has the Behold Factor, that presence that seems to fill up a room, overshadowing everything else that's going on. When he speaks, his voice is just a little louder than anyone else's, his laughter seems to override every joke, and his cologne permeates the space, no matter what fragrances others are wearing.

"Behold!" and everyone stops and looks his direction. It's as if we have no choice.

What does that mean in the real world? How does our Behold God fit into our everyday plans?

Well, in John 13:27, at the Last Supper, after the devil entered into Judas Iscariot, Jesus' Behold Factor came out loud and clear in the words he spoke to Judas.

> "What you are going to do, do it quickly."

Jesus knew exactly what was going on with his upcoming betrayal. He had predicted it, and he was resigned to seeing it carried out.

Later, in Acts 1:20, we read of the desolation that befell Judas after his horrendous act of betrayal. Verses 18-19 tell the story of Judas' horrific death, and then Peter quotes from the Book of Psalms.

> "May his camp become desolate, and let there be no one to dwell in it," and, "Let another take his office."

The Behold Factor here lies with the words of the psalmist, for the truth the world would deny rings out over the centuries. The Christ was crucified, and his usurper paid the ultimate price. Another shall now take the usurper's place.

In John 19:14, even Pilate spoke words of truth, although he said them in jest.

"Behold your King!"

And the people cried, "We have no king but Caesar," calling out, "Crucify him!"

Even so, Jesus had the best Behold moment of all. Read in Matthew 28:6, where the angel speaks to Mary Magdalene and the other Mary:

"He is not here, for he has risen, as he said. Come, see the place where he lay."

What is our Behold moment in our modern day world? How does the Behold Factor apply now?

Nothing has changed. It's the same as Paul's words in Romans 1:16:

"For I am not ashamed of the gospel, for it is the power of God for salvation to everyone who believes, to the Jew first and also to the Greek."

Every moment of every day can be a Behold moment for us. All we need to do is get hold of the Behold Factor and let it fill us up to overflowing.

The Behold Factor is Jesus, and he wants to come to

us to live inside our hearts forever and forever.

We can have him. All we have to do is accept his invitation. We find that in the Bible.

In summary, when our words come from Jesus, they carry power we could never speak on our own.

Light Bulb Moment

In God we never find sinking sand. Rather, he is the rock on which we stand.

The Concrete Wall

When we remodel a house, a concrete wall can be either a blessing or a curse.

If we pull down the plaster to discover concrete underneath, we can build anything we want on top. We have a support structure that will handle thousands of pounds. However, if we want to install a door or a window, then we must fall back on our jackhammer. It's a dusty, bone-jarring job in front of us.

God is our concrete wall. He is the beginning and the end, the great I Am that I Am, and the one on whom we must build to make heaven our home.

Here are four construction facts that guarantee our Christian success:

Fact #1:

> John 1:1 reminds us: "In the beginning was the Word, and the Word was with God, and the Word was God."

He is the start of every remodeling project. When we build on him, we build on a firm foundation.

Fact #2:

1 Corinthians 3:16 says: "Do you not know that you are God's temple and that God's Spirit dwells in you?"

When we build on God's foundation, we become a dwelling place for his spirit.

Fact #3:

Hebrews 4:12 cautions us: "For the word of God is living and active, sharper than any two-edged sword, piercing to the division of soul and of spirit, of joints and of marrow, and discerning the thoughts and intentions of the heart."

We will build true when we follow God's blueprints. He will blast through every bad thing we come against on our construction site.

Fact #4:

Ephesians 2:8-9 assures us: "For by grace you have been saved through faith. And this is not your own doing; it is the gift of God, not a result of works, so that no one may boast."

Our final product far exceeds what we can do in

ourselves. God is our construction foreman, and he knows just what he is doing.

Life is designed to align with God. When we choose to live in sin, we have to jackhammer past God to get there. He is always calling us, and he will be our firm foundation if we listen to him.

In summary, in God we never find sinking sand. Rather, he is the rock on which we stand.

Light Bulb Moment

When we come to God, we caress his heart with our presence, and he knows the joy of our love.

The Knife Plunged Into Our Heart

Our heart is a muscle and nothing more. It beats 100,000 times a day with the same force as giving a tennis ball a good squeeze.

Our heart keeps us alive with little complaint or extra effort on our part. We never see it, only sense it in times of extreme physical activity, and place our trust in it every single day that we walk the face of God's earth.

We hardly know it's there.

Yet, we say our heart is breaking; our heart is sad; love resides in our heart. What do we mean by all this?

We are speaking of our emotions, of course. The muscle in our chest responds to our emotions, but it is no more than a muscle; a fist-sized knot of pulsing energy that pumps gallon after gallon of blood through our body, keeping us healthy and strong for a lifetime.

So, a knife plunged into our heart is really the pain of sundered emotions. We hurt, we grab our chest, and we double over in pain.

Still, our heart beats, and we continue to draw in breath. We live, even as the pain consumes us.

What pain consumes God?

John 3:16 is the lynchpin of the Bible.

> "For God so loved the world, that he gave his only Son, that whoever believes in him should not perish but have eternal life."

> The very thought of his creation leaping to their destruction pained God enough that he gave up his most precious possession, his son, to give us the opportunity to come to him.

Romans 6:23 lays out the choice we are given.

> "For the wages of sin is death, but the free gift of God is eternal life in Christ Jesus our Lord."

> When we choose our own way, God's heart is torn with sorrow. His one desire is for us to turn to him.

Romans 3:23 is the wall that no human can get past.

"For all have sinned and fall short of the glory of God."

God cannot help who he is, for by his very nature, his glory shines forth from his holy throne. Even so, he looks past that and reaches his hand unto us.

Matthew 25:41 reveals the moment of God's utter devastation.

"Then he will say to those on his left, 'Depart from me, you cursed, into the eternal fire prepared for the devil and his angels.' "

He does not send the wicked from him with glee. Rather, he is cut to the core that some would choose to follow the paths of evil.

Revelation 21:8 lists that which crushes God's heart.

"But as for the cowardly, the faithless, the detestable, as for murderers, the sexually immoral, sorcerers, idolaters, and all liars, their portion will be in the lake that burns with fire and sulfur, which is the second death."

Remember, these are God's own creation. He is watching his children, having made their choices, be destroyed painfully and with no further chance for redemption.

Luke 22:44 is the broken heart of God.

> "And being in an agony he prayed more earnestly; and his sweat became like great drops of blood falling down to the ground."

> Yes, this passage refers to Jesus' desperate desire to avoid the pain of the cross. Even more, it tells us of his willingness to endure that pain so that humanity could know the rescuing hand of God the Father, lifting them up from their sin and despair.

We know the knife that plunges into our hearts. It is betrayal, love cast aside, and disregard for the relationships that make up our lives.

It is the same knife that plunges into the heart of God. It is why he sent Jesus for our redemption, so that we could salve that wound and let his love flow forth once more.

In summary, when we come to God, we caress his heart with our presence, and he knows the joy of our love.

Light Bulb Moment

When we cry out to Jesus, he will astonish us with his outpouring of love, and we will become one with him.

The Story of Astonishing Wonders

Let's weave an amazing tale. It's going to be better than Alice falling through a rabbit hole, more fantastic than Jack climbing a magical beanstalk, and will challenge the out-of-this-world feats of a man coming from a foreign planet as a baby to gain superpowers under our yellow sun.

It will be a story of astonishing wonders.

The story starts in the blackness of nothing. No sun, no earth, no moon, no space. The universe is a blank canvas lacking even entropy, with the canvas free of the existence of matter or energy.

Then, an astonishing wonder occurs. "In the beginning, God created the heavens and the earth." Genesis 1:1.

Life appeared out of nothingness, with planets, suns,

and all the stars in the heavens. It wasn't, and then it was, just like that.

The tale continues the story of God's creation, with the men who wander upon the face of the earth doing as they please, whether for themselves or for God. In the course of events, God realizes things are not working, for only one man still recognizes the Supreme Father and does what is right in his sight.

Then, an astonishing wonder occurs. "For behold, I will bring a flood of waters upon the earth to destroy all flesh in which is the breath of life under heaven." Genesis 6:17.

Only Noah and his family survive. The world has been given a fresh start, one designed after the true plan of God.

Man, though, is Man, and he has trouble remembering the divine nature of God. Once again humanity gets lost, chasing after his own desires rather than reaching for the hand of the Almighty God.

Then, an astonishing wonder occurs. "For God so loved the world, that he gave his only Son, that whoever believes in him should not perish but have eternal life." John 3:16.

God could have written mankind off and started afresh, but instead he offered us something more precious than silver and gold. He gave us himself, coming to live on the earth in human form in the person of Jesus.

There are many more wonders in this magnificent story. Jesus cried, "Peace! Be still!" in Mark 4:39, and the winds and the waves ceded to his command. Jesus spoke to the blind man, and "he recovered his sight" in Luke 18:43. The Holy Spirit came upon the believers, and they "began to speak in other tongues" in Acts 2:4.

These wonders lead us to the most astonishing wonder of all. We read Jesus' words in Luke 23:43. "Truly, I say to you, today you will be with me in Paradise." Our Lord may have been speaking to the condemned man who hung on the cross at his side, but the specific events recorded in the Word of God are not there by chance. This pivotal scene exemplifies the entire salvation message, giving it to us in one brief, emotional vignette of incredible beauty.

The thief had been very wicked, and he deserved to die. More to the point, he was already consumed in the throes of death, and he had no way to save himself. In his desperation, he found the shining light of Jesus' goodness, and he cried out to him.

That's all it took, crying out to Jesus with an earnest heart, and everything changed. The thief received the promise of Jesus, of salvation, and of life everlasting with the Father in Eternal Glory.

That is the most astonishing wonder in any story ever told.

In summary, when we cry out to Jesus, he will astonish us with his outpouring of love, and we will become one with him.

Light Bulb Moment

Jesus writes his truth on the whiteboard of the ages, so that we can draw unto him, learning to become like him.

Whiteboard of Truth

Chalkboards used to be all the rage. High technology, too. Those green expanses found in classrooms all across the nation served as our computer screens of the 20th century. We could load all the information we wanted, and with a swipe of our hand, we wiped it clean.

Then came the overhead projector, and we could save our lessons. Write them on acetate sheets, and when the lesson was over, they were gone, dropped into a folder for future reference.

Projectors needed a screen, though.

The whiteboard bridged the two. It wouldn't accept chalk. Rather, we had to purchase special markers that went on wet and dried to an erasable residue that held its shape until we wiped it off.

The one thing white boards were especially good for was a blank projector screen for that overhead projector, movies, or anything we wanted to shine that direction.

Of course, whiteboards have given way to computer-controlled Smart Boards, television screens, and computer monitors now, but in their heyday, they were cutting edge, and everyone wanted them.

The whiteboard presents two opportunities to illustrate Christ in our lives.

Illustration #1:

> The real difference between the whiteboard and a chalkboard is the residue that remains when the words and diagrams are removed. Erase a chalkboard, and the powdery remains of lessons taught stick to our hands and shower our legs and feet. And those who might be allergic? They will cough and sneeze, and the day will become a nightmare of misery.
>
> When we erase a whiteboard, there is no residue. Our hands stay clean, and everyone, allergies or not, breathes well for the rest of the day.
>
> One other thing to consider is that when the whiteboard is erased, everything is completely gone. The surface of the board is like new again, as if it has never been used at all.

That's what Christ does for us.

2 Corinthians 5:17 says, "Therefore, if anyone is in Christ, he is a new creation. The old has passed away; behold, the new has come."

When Christ wipes us clean, we are brand new. We cannot find any residue of life's cruel lessons anywhere on our person. It's all gone.

Illustration #2:

Our second illustration concerns the purpose of the whiteboard. It is, by design, meant to be loaded up with knowledge.

The knowledge is not static, though. It doesn't go on the board just for decoration. Rather, it is an avenue for transferring that knowledge to the unlearned among us.

1 Timothy 2:4 says, "Who desires all people to be saved and to come to the knowledge of the truth."

Our salvation is more than one simple act. Coming to Jesus is the first step, yes, but it starts a process that lasts our entire life. We have to ask ourselves, how do we maintain our salvation and grow to become like our Lord?

The answer is simple. We come to the knowledge of the truth. That knowledge is found in our study time with God's Word and in our teaching time under God's anointed teachers and ministers.

Unlike the more modern computer monitor, which is filled with knowledge but is blanked at the touch of a button, the whiteboard can hold the words we need to read for as long as we need them there.

When God has lessons for us to learn, his patience is infinite. He will work with us until we have come to his truth, and he will only wipe the board when we are with him in the glorious by and by.

In summary, Jesus writes his truth on the whiteboard of the ages, so that we can draw unto him, learning to become like him.

Coming to Christ
In Three Easy Steps

If you do not know Christ as your personal savior, there is no better time than the present to turn your life over to him.

➢ Step 1 is to admit that you are human, God is God, and you need his grace.

➢ Step 2 is to place your belief in him. You must accept that he is the Son of the Eternal God, and through his death on the cross, he can give you new life.

➢ Step 3 is to turn from your previous ways and receive the hope of Jesus' power in you.

Fill in the following information as a testament to your decision to accept Jesus as your Savior.

I, _____, accept Jesus
       print your full name

as my personal savior on _____.
                                today's date

_____
        your signature

Look for these additional topics on the MyChurchNotes.net website:

2 Timothy
Beatitudes
Discipleship
Evangelism
Faith
Family
Healing
Hope
Kingdom of God
Money
Prayer
Relationships
Repentance
Salvation
Worship

MyChurchNotes.net is a faith-based ministry founded on a belief in the Father, the Son, and the Holy Spirit. All MyChurchNotes.net articles are based on Scripture and created especially for MyChurchNotes.net.

Our Mission Statement is to take the Word of God into all the nations, and proclaim that he is Lord!

If you enjoyed
God Is Salvation for a Lost World,
please visit us at our website:

www.MyChurchNotes.net

We look forward to hearing from you.

Website and Publication Powered by:

Bright Herd . . . for All Your Website and Media Design Needs.
www.brightherd.com
contact@brightherd.com